How 1

Guide On Tiny House Building

Introduction

With the dramatic increase in the cost and reduced availability of space, it's no surprise that alternatives to traditional homes have gained in popularity. This new normal have given rise to the latest craze in the real estate market, Tiny Houses, but this development is one that might actually benefit your wallet. If building your own Tiny House is your goal, you'll need the resources and guidance on where to start as well as the tools on how to complete your Tiny House on a budget and without the headache of unexpected legal and material time and cost.

Chapter 1 – Getting Started

Now that you've decided that you want to build you own Tiny House, the next logical question is where do you begin? For something as complex as building a home, even a tiny one, the first step is to plan. The best way start planning is to organize your plan and start by looking at the following items: 1. zoning, permits, and other legalities, 2. location, 3. complexity and required labor, 4. existing plans and other resources, and 5. materials and supplies.

No matter what the task, it is recommended to you start your planning with an organized approach by making a physical and/or digital folder for each step and resource along the way. This will make it easier for you in case you get lost as well as help you pace out time in incremental and easy to follow steps. Once you have your outline ready, you will need to look into which permits will be required and where you can construct your tiny house. This means you need to research zoning laws as well as building permits and requirements for the location where you plan on building your structure.

State and local laws are not the only consideration. If your land is part of an association, there are usually additional restrictions that can include numerous limitations on shape, size, color, or type of construction allowed. You may even be required to ask for permission before you start your project. You will also need to acquire additional permits for different aspects of your projects such as electrical, plumbing, cable, and even noise. Just remember that the type of permit and permission you need will vary greatly depending on your location and municipality. It may even vary based on the cost and size of your Tiny House, so take those aspects into consideration during your research process. While rules and permits will change with time and location, the internet has simplified the research process for you. Most of the time you can do a simple search that includes +rules +permits +"tiny house" +"insert your town here" in just about any search engine.

After you have looked into the legal requirements for your desired location, you should also compare the restrictions with other areas you may be considering. Urban locations tend to have significantly more requirements that rural areas, so sometimes simply moving a short distance outside of a legal boundary of an urban area my lessen the regulatory burden of your endeavor. Once you have compared requirements for several different locations, you will want to investigate both the complexity and the time requirements of the job. If you are planning on constructing the Tiny House all by yourself or with the help of friends and family, you want to be fully aware of how long it will take and what you need before you begin. The importance of this cannot be overstated. People often forget that time is money. Even if you are retired, you could be spending your time on something else every moment that you are building or planning your Tiny House. Expect delays as well as cost and time overruns. Don't be afraid to ask other's who finished their own project how long it might take or what unexpected delays and expenses popped up during the process. This will also vary with location and plan, so ask people in your area for projects similar to the one you are planning.

Your next step will be to research existing plans and sources. Luckily for you, we have included some plans as well as links for additional plans and sources to help you along the way. The final step in your planning process will be to acquire the materials needed for the construction of your home. This includes any tools you may need to modify or prepare your raw materials. The raw materials you select for your home should also be ideal for your region and your plan. Consider how different types of wood and metal stand up the the elements in your desired location and what other people have used for similar projects.

There is also a cost consideration. You will find that you get what you pay for. By spending a little more in the beginning for better quality materials, you may save money in the long run through repairs and added durability. Now that we've discussed how to begin, the next sections will focus on various styles of homes, and main aspects of their construction.

Chapter 2 – Resources

Most people are attracted to the idea of a tiny house for either the reduced cost or the simpler lifestyle. One should not assume, however, that all Tiny Houses will be cheap or that they will necessarily simplify your life. You can, however, get a good comparison in the Tiny Life resource guide (http://thetinylife.com/what-is-the-tiny-house-movement/). Nevertheless, you will want to make use of all the available resources to insure that you the type of home you build and the process itself saves time and cost without sacrificing quality or cutting legal corners.

Two additional things that need to be addressed are resale value and ambiguity in zoning laws. Resale value is generally lower than traditional homes, so be aware of this when planning on construction, investment, and retirement. Tiny Houses are also sometimes unclassified as a structure. This complicates permitting and fines. It's better to be proactive by inquiring prior purchasing land or materials. Hopefully, the resources provided will help with some of these issues.

It's nearly impossible to talk about Tiny Houses without bringing up one of the forerunners in the industry, Jay Shafer. His book (http://www.fourlightshouses.com/products/the-small-house-book-paperback) is not free, but it does provide an excellent resource for planning, zoning, efficiency as well as examples of various relevant and related structures. The great thing about looking at his experience and history is that you become familiar with some of the biggest issues related to Tiny Houses. There are a few other places where you can find resources on legal requirements. One of my favorite sites includes a checklist website (http:// thetinylife.com/ryans-tiny-house/tiny-house-building-checklist/), which contains not only zoning and permitting tips, but also a good planning outline. Another great source for information is a community based site (http://tinyhousecommunity.com/faq.htm) that serves as a FAQ for topics related to the subject.

In addition to planning resources, also consider material resources that keep you from building from scratch. While a typical Tiny House may cost you around $40K, there are ways cut that in less than half. Take for example, Macy Miller (http://www.thetinyhouse.net/this-could-be-the-trailer/), who used a rough trailer to bring the total cost down to less than $12K.   There are also more extreme examples (http://www.desmoinesregister.com/story/life/2015/02/02/tiny-house-central-college-students/22777267/) of how very basic design constructions, when combined with significant do it yourself man power, have been built using less than $500. Keep in mind, though, that this is not typical and such examples are generally only partially functioning.

Chapter 3 – Plans

I have included a basic plans from from the source listed in the link below, but you will also want to keep in mind that you may need to modify plans based on your own needs. This can include changes based on using portions of preexisting constructions, trailers, or recycled materials. If you are more advanced, you may consider combining aspects of different plans for cost or design preference. In addition to the plans listed below, you can find numerous sites for free plans including this one (http://www.tinyhousedesign.com/free-plans/) as well as The plan shown below can also be downloaded (http://cdn2.tinyhousedesign.com/wp-content/uploads/2009/04/8x8-tiny-house-plans-v3.pdf) direct from tinyhousedesign.com and boasts not only the complete blue print, but also the list of materials at a total cost of $2,000 (excluding finishing, trip, plumbing, & eletrical). It also suggest that the actual construction of the plan will run as much as $6,000. The plan is a simply 8 by 8 plan of a Tiny House.

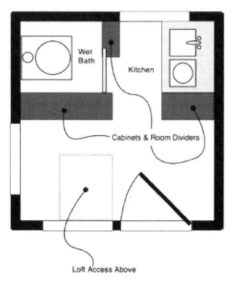

Wet Bath

Kitchen

Cabinets & Room Dividers

Loft Access Above

As shown above the floor plan is just one of many possible choices for an 8 by 8 setup. The interior walls and built in cabinets of this particular plan make use of the existing structure to maximize space, something you must consider when finalizing your design. The loft can also be reached from above the ground. The next image from the same blueprint illustrates the diagram of the floor framing. Notice the to plywood used on the lower section of the illustration. This depicts the concept that you do not want the actual floor structure touching the ground. You should use piers or even concrete to support the structure itself.

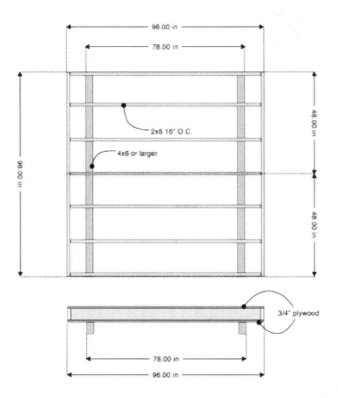

Next we have the back wall and front wall. You can see the framing of the windows and doors, but these can be adjusted as needed.

Back Wall

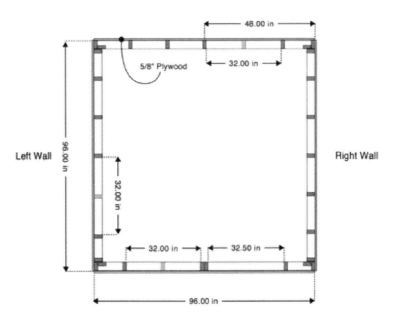

Left Wall

Right Wall

Front Wall

12

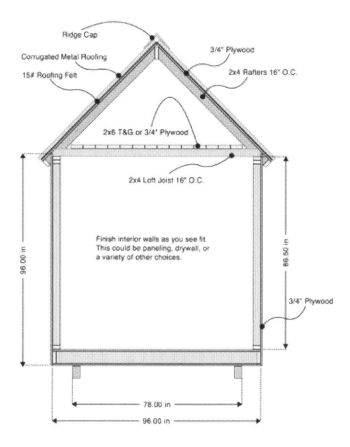

In the cross section, you see what happens with the house is divided in half. This does not include any insulation, so you will need to add this on your own. Thick lumber and groove plywood are ideal for the construction of the loft.

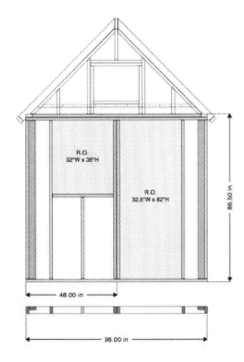

Next we have the front and back wall framing plans. A double top plate is used as support, and there are no headers on the windows and doors. This particular plan makes use of the existing wall height with works well with the exterior sheathing.

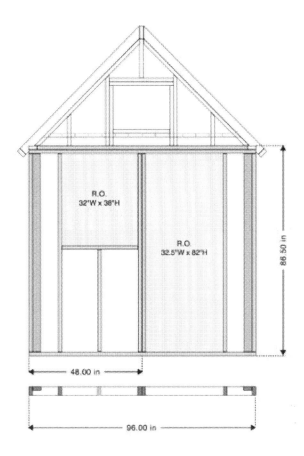

The two diagrams show below illustrate the left and right wall framing. Once again, windows and doors are easily moved along this plan. Also, take not of the 2 by 4's positioned along the edges.

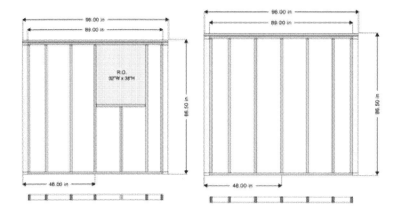

The final two diagrams show the loft framing plan and the roof framing. Both show how light and ventilation are provided by the loft area. Again, all illustrations depicted are taken from tinyhousedesign.com with the full floor plan and materials available to and first list above. In addition to the plans laid out here, you can also find numerous sources of free plans, or inexpensive sketch up plans such as those listed here (http://www.thesmallhousecatalog.com/free-plans/).

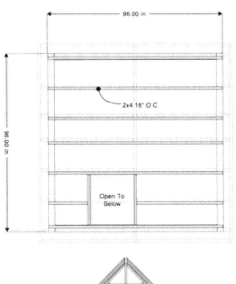

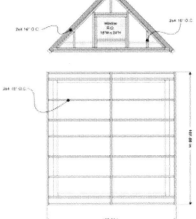

17

Chapter 4 – Materials

Once you've decided on the final plan, the next step is to begin acquiring materials. By this point, though, you should at least know what type of materials you are going to need for the main structure, whether is lumber, concrete, or some other material. You should know where you can purchase materials in your area, but I would also highly recommend that you get creative in your approach to get supplies. Don't be afraid to ask around, whether it be at a recycling center, construction area, or other job sites. Sometimes you will find unused material that others would be willing to give you if you just have the courage to ask.

Along those same lines, think outside the box when it comes to recyclables. I've seen numerous examples of reclaimed shipping containers (http:// www.criticalcactus.com/shipping-container-homes/) that were turned into quarters or smaller components that were used as walls or floors. Whether you use glass bottles, salvaged metals, recycled wood, pallets, you will find a host of options to choose from. Just take a look at here (http://www.criticalcactus.com/beautiful-recycled-homes/). One of the great features regarding recyclables or reclaimed materials is that it allows you to get creative with your design. Traditional materials are often more rigid and require a certain consistency in order to fit the specific blueprint or plan. If you use alternative materials, you can take an existing plan and modify it a little or a lot based on the supplies that you have.

In addition to design flexibility, alternative materials and designs also have the added benefit of incorporating sustainable options such as heat conservation, which can reduce power needs. They can also simply the building process and reduce the time and cost requirements. Finding alternative or recycled materials for your construction does not have to be a difficult process either. You can find numerous places that offer several sources of those materials such as here (http://www.treehugger.com/tiny-houses/learn-build-tiny-house-salvaged-building-materials.html) and here (http://tinyhousetalk.com/how-to-get-reclaimed-materials-for-your-tiny-house/). There is now even a classes you can take on how to learn to salvage and mine materials for whatever structure it is that you want to build.

If you do decide on more traditional materials, you'll have no shortage of places to find what you need. The biggest challenge, though, will be will finding the best value and most consistent product. Fourlighthouses (http://www.fourlightshouses.com/pages/cost-to-build) offers many of the prefabricated components including trailers, foundations, and trim. It also has cost estimates, which is handy. You can also find another traditional source of rated, though a bit pricey, materials and supplies here (http://tinyhousegiantjourney.com/tiny-house-materials/). If you do decided on more traditional sources, be very aware of the cost. Fixtures and windows can get very expensive quickly, so one option may be to purchase traditional supplies for the bulk of your foundation, but use recycled windows, doors, and fixtures to save on some of the more pricey items.

Chapter 5 – Trailer

After your materials are selected, your next step will be to decide on a trailer or foundation. Trailers can give the added advantage of allowing you to get around building or zoning restrictions, but check before you decide. If you can make use of a recycled trailer, all the better. If not, you still have several options. You can find pre made trailers beginning at around $1500 here (http://tinyhousebasics.com/trailers/), as well as additional options here (https://www.tinyhomebuilders.com/tiny-house-trailers/build-your-trailer). Of course, the design of your Tiny House will determine the size and type of your trailer. If you have a smaller house, you can get away with a smaller trailer. If you have no idea where to begin with deciding on what you need for your trailer, start here (http://tinyrevolution.us/2010/10/15/what-kind-of-trailer-to-buy-for-a-tiny-house/).

There is also the option of making your own trailer. If cost is your biggest concern, then this may be your best option. New trailers can average between $3000 to $6000, so constructing your own can significantly reduce the cost.

Chapter 6 – Foundation

Trailers are not the only option, and while they may help you avoid certain building codes, there are some good reasons to opt for the foundation over the trailer. One of the key reasons to go with a foundation is that you have added flexibility in the design of your Tiny House. Working with trailers requires that you build on an existing frame. There is little room for building outside of that literal box, even if it is just a few inches. The foundation avoids that issue.

The foundation can be as simple as a concrete slab, but you can also have a happy medium by selecting runners, piers, or skids. This option allows you the flexibility of using a temporary, semi-permanent foundation that might also allow you the same option as a trailer in terms of avoiding building codes and permits. Here (http://www.thetinyhouse.net/skip-the-trailer-13-tiny-houses-built-on-foundations/) is a great resource for such an option, which looks at 13 different homes built on semi-permanent foundations.

Chapter 7 – Frame, Sheathing, Windows, Doors

Once you have either a foundation or trailer, the next step will be to build the bulk of your main structure. This includes a sturdy frame along with sheathing, windows, doors, and finally a roof. The type of each component will depend on the actual sketch or design that you select, but there are a few rules or tips that you can use to help you along the way for each section. For your frame, a simple 2 by 4 option is the most common, but this choice can make insulation a challenge. You will also want to consider weight, cost, strength, and complexity when deciding on your frame. Some alternative to traditional framing include advanced framing, steel studs, aluminum framing, as well as engineered framing and trusses. Tinyhousetalk (http://tinyhousetalk.com/framing-tiny-houses/) has an excellent write up and alternative framings.

Sheathing is another major component in your construction. This step also requires that you check for errors and will largely depend on your particular floor plan. Make sure you spend the necessary time on this step, otherwise, when you get to the windows and doors you may need to redo all your work. Save yourself the hassle and double check each step along the way. Be sure to measure and check your beams. See to it that your corners are aligned. Don't wing it or eyeball it, be as accurate as possible.

Now that you have finished the hard part, your next step is to install your windows and doors. You do have some flexibility in the step, and can even make some last minute changes, especially if you used wood sheathing. Of course you will need to frame your windows and doors first. This can be one of the more enjoyable aspects of the job, but don't forget about your insulation! Different window and door types will require different types of insulation, so pay close attention.

As your Tiny House nears completion, you will need to build your roof. I recommend going with a vaulted roof and a higher ceiling for reasons I'll mention later in the book, but regardless, you want to make sure that you roof is solidly constructed and leak proof. This means you not only want to make sure that it is sturdy, but you also want to think carefully about the materials used on the outside of your roof such as tiling or shingles. Asphalt shingles are not very wind resistant, and ceramic is heavy, so consider metal roofing, which is a very popular choice. Another option is 3d shingles known as Ondura. You can find a more

detailed explanation of Ondura shingles here (http://tinyhousegiantjourney.com/
2014/06/14/roofing/).

Once you've gotten to this point, you house is coming together and looks about
complete, but there are still lots of considerations for the furnishings and
finishing touches. Before you start adding your furnishings, though, this is where
you double check everything. Make sure you fully insulated your entry points and
roof. If there are any major mistakes that you overlooked, it's better you find
them now before you start adding your appliances or furnishings.

Once you've double checked your major components, decide on whether or not
you want staining, paint, or some type of siding for you finishing touches. This
will have a major impact on how you decorate the inside of your new home.

Chapter 8 – Additional Tips & Furnishings

There are numerous things that can help ease the potential problems of building
a Tiny House. One such consideration that is often overlooked is the time of year
that the home is constructed. One such example, shown below, is of a couple who
realized that building during periods of cold and rain can prove problematic. The
solution to that problem is building during times of the year when it is warm and
dry. You may not realize it, but if you build during times of inclement weather, a
headache is not your only concern. You can add significant cost and time to your
build. If you aren't sure when the wettest time of year is in your region, consult an
online farmers almanac and weather site that gives climatological statistics on
rain days.

Deciding on the best time of year to build your Tiny House is not your only consideration. One of the key factors when designing your house after the general blueprint is chosen, is how to maximise space. The can be accomplished by using fold down options for numerous added features such as beds, benches, dining tables, and appliances. Another method of utilizing existing space is by using existing wall space for added functionality. Kitchens are especially suited for using wall space more effectively for utensils and other items. You can find a great article on wall storage here (http://www.home-storage-solutions-101.com/wall-storage.html).The use of wall space doesn't have to be limited to small items either. Entire dual functioning walls are possible if you get creative enough with your design.

While dual functionality is a plus, you also want to keep a clutter free feeling in your new home. This can be accomplished by keeping those wall hangings and other items on the lower third of your wall. Combine that with high ceilings and you maximise storage, functionality, as well as the feeling of added space. Using a combined bathroom and shower is another item that is often overlooked. Y o u can also use the toilet down as a dual functioning seat, while in the shower. Along

24

the same concept, you will want to make use of tools such as added mirrors, windows, and lighting, all three of which can add a surprising feel of added space. You will also want to avoid partitions, which make a home feel smaller and disconnected from the rest of the home.

While you work at multipurpose walls, you should also consider multipurpose furniture such as beds. Sliding compartments are similar feature that can add more space. One such bed, shown below, doubles as a desk. Using space underneath stairs is another creative option as well for adding storage.

http://
tinyhousetalk.com/small-space-furniture-20-multipurpose-beds/

In addition to beds, there is also the option of book cases and storage containers that adjust to fit your needs. You can even find options such as kitchen tables that double as pool tables. Whether is work or play, you can find almost an infinite number of dual and multi function appliances that suit your needs. Many of these can be purchased, but if you are building your home from scratch, you may even consider looking up some design for making your own multi functioning furniture and appliances. While all of the aforementioned features can add both real and perceived space, don't forget that you still might need actual storage, so be sure to make room somewhere for that storage space. Adding a deck can also help with both additional storage and perceived extra space.

We've discussed ways to maximise space, but you should never stop looking. It is also highly likely that you will end of finding a better way to be more efficient with your space AFTER you already have your design and have started building. In that instance, don't be afraid to modify or change your design. There is no reason why you can't change it after the fact. The only consideration is if you are willing to put in the extra time and money, if any, that is needed to make the alteration.

I also recommend that you make use of solar panels for power. This is a necessity if you are off grid, but it can also be a life safer in an emergency when the power goes out. Depending on your location, your local power company may reach you much later than urban or semi urban areas, and having a source of power that is not dependent on regular power lines is very helpful. Another VERY important tip that we haven't discussed much is safety. I not just talking about theft, I am referring to injury prevention. If you are building the home yourself or enlisting the help of others, you want to make sure that everyone is following safe building practices. This includes using the proper equipment. Making sure the equipment and tools are working properly and being used correctly. Also use safety goggles, gloves, and other safety devices when doing any type of cutting or use of equipment that can present any type of hazard. This also means installing fire extinguishers and smoke detectors.

Chapter 9 – You Have A Plan, Now What?

After reading this book, there are still several things that you will need to do and consider. The first of those is money. As mentioned in the beginning, your labor is valuable. Also expect that the project will take longer than you anticipate. If you go into a project with that understanding, you will save yourself unnecessary headaches. With time in mind, you will want to plan smartly in the beginning. Going back to step one, you want to streamline your planning process as much as possible. This includes organizing your planning in a simple and logical way, and making sure that your information is backed up in case of a mishap.

Once you have moved beyond the first stages, you also want to consider maintenance and security. Your new house may be small, but it's still subject to normal wear and tear, and it also has it's own unique issues related to security. This can include both damage from natural disasters as well as theft. Look into insurance, security, and common maintenance issues before you begin spending any money. Make sure that you have thoroughly exhausted your research on all legal requirements. Unfortunately, you may not find a one stop shop for all your legal needs for free, and the rules are ever changing. You should also anticipate the possibility of what might happen if you unexpectedly run afoul of the law. Perhaps the best way to prepare for such an eventuality is by purchasing legal insurance. While research and planning will go a long way in limiting potential legal problems, one cannot prevent all legal challenges, and an inexpensive liability or legal policy may be worth considering, if only for the added peace of mind. If you're not sure where to start, you can look at policies (https:// www.legalshield.com/) that start from as little as $20 a month.

When it comes time to actually start your planning and keeping, there are several things that can help ease the process. This includes imagining the work in your mind being completed. Having an image in your head is an excellent motivator. You also want to recognize when you are spent. If you are exhausted and need a break, take one. Having a day off or two when you need it will make you more efficient with your time when you are working and make the process a lot more enjoyable. Along those lines, you also want to make sure that you are taking care of yourself. Get plenty of rest, and live healthy. You need both your physical and mental strength, so do want you must in order to maintain it.

Along your adventure, invite those that you care about to share in your experience, even if it is just to visit. There is no need to isolate yourself from those you care about while working on your project. Make them part of your memories, and keep doing what you enjoy doing, whether that's listening to music or hanging out with friends. I cannot promise that everything will go smoothly along the way, but if you plan well, this should help mitigate some of those potential pitfalls. Make sure that you plan, plan, and plan. Create a to do list to break up larger sections of the job into more manageable chunks.

No matter how well you planned, or how realistic you set your expectations, there will always be times when things go run. You will have time and cost overruns, missing or damaged materials. You will forget things, have to reschedule things, make mistakes, and make other misshaps. During those time, you just need to accept the fact that those issues are part of the process. While it can be frustrating and tiring when it is happening to you in the moment, that time will eventually pass. Stick with it, and get the job done.

Don't be afraid to reach out to others who have worked on similar projects. Find out people who live in their own Tiny House and what issues they learned during planning, construction, and living. Be aware of things like resale value and issues with moving. Become familiar with every facet of the job and the lifestyle before you begin, and you will greatly enhance your chances of a successful process.

One final note, I recommend having a reason for building your home before you begin. This is perhaps the most important step of the entire process because it should influence nearly every decision you will have to make. Is it to save money, to simplify, or some other purpose? Make sure you understand that reason, and have it written down before you begin. Come back to it at different times of the planning process. Look at it during your build. If you know why you are building it then it will be easier to decide what you need. Whether it's kitchen space, entertainment, or some other functionality, function should inform from not the other way around.

Conclusion

While starting the task of constructing your own home can seem frightening, it doesn't have to be. Planning well and following a clear path that includes resources for support and a step by step outline will take the mystery and fear out of getting starting on your dream of building your own Tiny House. If you follow through with the formula of researching and planning, you'll find that your goal of a Tiny House on a budget is both exciting and achievable.

Manufactured by Amazon.ca
Bolton, ON